The Girl Who Never Got Written

By Terri Lee-Shield

Dedicated to all the souls who supported my healing journey.
Thank you I am forever grateful.

And especially to:

Vicky Woodruff

Who's hands filled my heart with love when I had been surrounded by darkness for so long I had forgotten such tenderness could exist.

ISBN: 9798840577936

Foreword

The Girl Who Never Got Written is a collection of poetry, prose & word art that has flown from me and through me as I embarked on a healing journey.

As the sentimental child in a northern family who seemed to never ask the questions I was born wondering. I could never find the words I needed to express myself well. I didn't have the knowledge or the skill. I was never really introduced to writing as a form of expression or art. But I wanted to.

I always had this idea I would write a book. That one day I would keep a diary (or dairy as I first named my handmade school project) that devastated me and further stunted my embarkment upon this desire of mine.

When I did start a diary I had no idea what I wanted to write. I knew I wanted to record my life. To have an account of all these experiences, questions, feelings, notions and things I noticed that no one but me seemed to care about. But when I started one all I could muster were the words I thought my friends would want me to write about Brian Davies and Paul Charlton. Or the fear my mother would find and the knowing she would most definitely read it. And I would forget I had started one and miss the opportunity to write again the next day.

My diary always ended with little of interest and a sense of disappointed and failure n myself.

But the words were still there. The questions, the beauty, the fears all unexpressed and contained, kept in the vault of my memory of mind knowing that one day as an adult I would write them out. My adulthood came and I never did. I was too busy. It wasn't what grown ups did. Until I killed myself and failed at that too.

When I woke as a shaken soul I had to make a change and I made a pretty radical one. I decided to commit to my spirituality, heal, give meaning and explore these ideas and questions I held as a child bu ignored and rejected after trauma.

Once I started to go to spiritual healing words became to come to me sometimes. In the form of poetry. Untrained, untamed and without editing. I started to write them down. Over time my journaling developed and I became more skilled with words, I developed my language, consider semantics, became the author I had wanted to be as a small child stifled by my lack of growth.

Now I write and publish often. Pretty much every day. I journal or create media content, blogs, books and sometimes the poetry comes. It flows to me and through me like a channel. I am the muse and the artist.

Last night was one of those nights. When words began to come and I could not settle for writing them. And today became the day I would publish them in this book. The Girl Who Never Got Written is my gift to the little girl that always wondered what words could mean. Who was curious if expression could make magic or indeed a difference. It is a book I am sharing to meet the child in you perhaps that wondered the same.

July 7th 2022.

In no particular order...

Today I have started a new book. Today I have started a new chapter. I have no idea what I will write, how or where I will write it or even how long it will take to write.

Will I ever finish it?

Will this be the conclusion of my experiment or the slow burn of beginning a reaction?

Diary, memoirs, novel, poetry, prose or inspiration...who knows what the beautiful blank pages of this book will become full of.

All I wish is that whatever it may be, let it be truth, love and learning for all.

Friday 17th October 2014

Words in Motion

The words that won't stop
They just want to flow,
With no where to put them
They've no where to go.

Who knows what truth they bring
If someone else sees them
Or how they might feel
By being near them.

The words are not mine
But they want to be written,
Perhaps an avid reader
Will love them, be smitten.

As words they can move us
With little context or cause
Without evoking our power
Or inviting a pause.

Words bring love or cause wars
Depending how they are used
But words have no meaning
Without the right muse.

Where a page was wide open
With unlimited potential
We have the ability to make light
Be harsh or truly gentle.

Words that mean nothing
Given no power or purpose,
Can move us to surrender
To the depths from our surface.

Dive in and discover
How these words move your motions
But remember the credit
Belongs only to your notions.

7.7.22

I Remember

I remember.

I remember the spirit I was before I needed spirituality.
I remember the woman I was becoming before I knew there was a
support available to me.
I remember the fire that burned when I was free from the binds of
trauma and experience.
I remember the bold, assertive and progressive young woman who
spoke out against injustice and prejudice without fear of a response.
I remember a world when media did not dictate my thoughts, my
world or my actions.
I remember a passion that was there without trying.
I remember her rawness.
Her untamed, smoking, swearing never apologetic outlook on life.
I remember who I was when I started life on my own terms.

I am not her I just remember how it felt to be her.
Now I am me.
I am more experienced.
I have more wisdom.
I need less caution.
I will not be put back in a box of conditions a box I was so pleased to
be free of.
A young woman who had no idea what life could do to her.
Is now a grown woman who does, who has lived and survived and
who remembers who she was.
Between me and the moon make no mistake.
We can not be contained and we we will not be explained.
You will not catch me caring about the conditions of my box again.
I was designed to think outside of it.
And I will

Pride and Shame

I had never really fully considered the relationship between pride
and shame.
I was never proud of my self often so unsure.
I had moments of being proud of what I created.
A moment of affirming my beauty.
But so confused also about the shame.
Was I bad?
I am both.
Good and bad.
Pure and dirty.
Clean and sinful.
I can love what I create.
But only because I love it and it was me in a real moment.
A moment that became physical.
It is the magic that I love.
No more pride.
No more shame.
Just love for what exists.
And acceptance that it dies.

7.7.22

May this retreat help to open my soul. May it develop my skills, expand my mind and enlighten my heart. May all that needs to be expressed be written. May all that should be lost forgotten.

[It was never lost, nor forgotten.]

Stop!

Stop telling me what to think or how I should feel.
Stop assuming what I know is not valid or real.
Stop telling me to respond different to how I am.
Stop expecting me to behave the same as you can.

Stop being the cause of me questioning my mind.
Stop assuming my view has been skewed or i'm blind.
Stop thinking my consideration has not taken me long.
Stop questioning my life and making me wrong.

Stop forcing my body to do what you what.
Stop behaving like monsters but pending you don't.
Stop being unkind and making others small.
Stop pretending it's fine and no problem at all.

There's nothing about me that needs to be changed...
I'm fucking awesome and they are deranged!

16.1.22

Rage and Burn

The rage I feel at what they did and has been done
The anger burns me deeply intense like the sun.
Anything I say or do, how I respond or feel.
Always questioned by others; is this real?

Who decides if I'm right or wrong
Certainly not a stranger who is there, then gone.
Why is my view never accepted?
Always assumed that its wrong and I'm less than.

I make no mistake in expressing what I see
It makes no difference what you think of me.
But defending abuse and the harm that is causes.
Denying the effects of rape on our daughters.

I don't blame you for denying or fearing the burn.
But it's not me who needs changed, only them.
The ones who dismiss the effect they have on others.
The ones who stay quiet defending their brothers.

I'll never sit down and accept its okay.
I'm not stupid enough to think it'll just go away.
I won't silence myself or numb my reaction.
I'm here to burn it up and cause decisive action!

16.1.22

Why do men have to be right, more than women get to be safe?

25.12.20

For Laura

To the girl who wishes
Not to be
Seen.
Standing in nature.
Layers of green.

To the girl who wishes
Not to be
Noticed.
Being herself.
No intention or motive.

To the girl who wishes
Only to
Hide.
Watching her.
My heart bursts with pride.

To the girl who wishes
Not to be
Visible.
Surely know.
For you it's not possible.

To the girl who wishes
Not to be
Seen.
Light Blinding.
Bright like a dream.

October 2014

Lost and Found

Sometimes you need to leave everything you know to truly find yourself. As you exist outside all you ave experienced you become who you truly are.

When the idea of your humanity becomes secondary to the pure soul that seeks to understand and experience.

And then when you return to all you once knew you realise you were only what you had been taught to become. You never really existed outside of the perceptions of others ideas of you.

Aside from the ground that always felt your changing weight and the air that you rejected each breath of your slumber.

7.7.22

My Gift

It was the thing I never wanted to see
It took the life I thought was meant for me
It prodded and poked me into deep silence
It showed me nothing good comes out of violence

It directed my path to places I would miss
It stole from me the joy of love or a first kiss
It warped who I was and all I could be
It shaped my mind so I could not be free.

It triggers my panic I go into a muddle
It makes some days feel like a big uphill struggle
The catalyst that inspired me to think for myself
So I wasn't some reject left on the shelf.

It leads me to behave in peculiar fashion
It directs my energy with clarity and passion
It brought be perspective and deep clear insight
It invites me to dance with life and not fight.

It opened me up to be all that I am
And challenges me to live the best way I can
It inspires my voice to stay true to my story
It gives me good reason to let go of power or glory

It filled me with fear and caused me to freeze up
It challenged me to choose when enough was enough
The wise heartless teacher that taught me it all
That striving too highly often leads to a fall

It lead me to loneliness into deep dark places
It taught me that people can't be judged by their faces
It lead me to search for truth near and far
It encouraged me to believe I could be a star.

The struggle that challenged all of my might
A friend that would guide me away from the light
It pulled me to places out of my range
It gave me perspective I would not change.

I'm put into boxes and told what I am,
My opinion considered trolling my perspective a sham,
I'm judged as defective my mentality flawed
So non truly see me and my uniqueness is ignored.

Its not that it's a gift my insightful way of seeing
It causes every connection to ripple through my being
To know and feel things others can skip past
I have to invest in relationships that don't seem to last.

For all that I am and all I've been given
To be stunted so young when I'd just started living
The gains I've accepted come at a price
Navigating through worry, trouble and strife.

My body so perfect was never adored,
I was denied a level of respect others can afford.
It fires up rage and bouts of great sadness
Makes me appear crazed deranged and filled with a madness.

The lesson that taught me to honour my health
The drive that allowed me to let go the pursuit of wealth
It melted my coldness from the fire arisen
It taught me the value of mistakes forgiven

The power I had would never be discovered
It became the friend that showed me strength uncovered
It gave me the space to find who I am
It made me unique and inspired my plans.

It gave my life meaning as I woke from deep slumber
It forced me to value myself and remember
It fills my heart with passion and purpose
It drives me to end competition and versus.

It invites me to consider there's no right or wrong
As it inspires my artwork, poetry and song
It builds my experience adds depth and understanding
It urges my up spin to consider its landing

It forces me to be comfortable alone in my place
It makes me aware of the value of space
Its not that it's wanted or I'm pleased for its purpose
It reminds me to consider no human is worthless

It out ideas exhaustive and big I my head
It left me with nothing I wanted to be dead
It drive me to search for what peace I could find
It challenged my nature and broke open my mind.

The events that weakened me and took away my power
Encouraged my growth to bloom like a flower
They gave me the taste of sorrow and took away my fun
And bright me to move to close to the sun

It provides for me good reason to pause and consider
How different life would be if it was all goodness without sinners
It took from me my unborn son and likely a daughter
But I would not be me without the pain of this life or my trauma.

10.1.22

Here I Am

Here I am...
Here I am in drizzly, misty, grey, colourful, Dhanakosa. Here I am looking for something. But what? I feel like I am here after having found myself, clarifying something perhaps, who knows? Do I even know?
My soul does but my body can never seem to find the exact words to describe what I am thinking or feeling. Yet here I am, ready to look, search, be accept, discover or whatever I happen to do whilst here.

I'm leaving behind....
I'm leaving behind my worry, stress and being hard on myself. I am leaving behind my quest for perfection...IT IS NEVER GOING TO HAPPEN! So why would I care if it isn't as I imagined or as good as I expect in my mind? Since it has never been before, why would I even want to control the outcome of something which was never meant to be perfect, only created and in fact by being imperfect is perfect because that is what it is.
I am leaving behind e the expectations and the worry and most of all I am letting go of the control (I think I had). Leaving behind the control freak. I'm leaving behind my fear.

I'm bringing...
I'm bringing a new attitude, a new adventure. I am bringing a new awareness. I am bringing fun and joy and compassion and empathy and acceptance and most of all love. I bring me. All of me. The real me. The happy me, the strong and stable me. The me that understands that good and bad exist only I my mind and I am bringing a soul that can deal with anything and act in love with strength and beauty like the universe reminds me to every day.

Here I hope to find...
Here I hope to find a true relief and release and flexibility and confirmation that my path is right. NO I DON'T!!
I already have this.
Here I hope to find whatever is in me that is lost, if anything. I hope to find perhaps a new way to express my soul.

17.10.14

My Gratitude

Today I am grateful for....
Long lazy lie ins and no wakeup alarm.
The day being planned for me but still having the choice about what I do.
Warm nutritious food coupled with warm nutritious conversation.
The freedom to explore my thoughts and the peace to sit and think.
The warm indoors and the cool outside.
The feel of rain on my face and the slip of grass at my feet.
The security of a boundary and the excitement of none.
Time.
Being able to do what I enjoy.
The opportunity to explore a new talent and skill.
The awareness to be able to better myself and my life.
Wise words.
Skilled teaching.
A warm bed.

18.10.14

The Cat

Cat never wonders
If the caught mouse
Pleases the farmer

October 2014

Subject to Change...Part 2

I am sitting int the same seat I have sat in many times before,
but it feels different.
I am looking at a view I have gazed at over many seasons,
Over many days.
But it does not look the same.

I watch a tree.
A tree that only this morning was fresh and new with it's glory of
colour.
It wants to stand steadfast, but it can not because the restless wind
will not let it rest.
A wind that will move each leaf to it's liking using a gust or a
breeze.

I notice an army of proud and strong darkened green firs.
They are clinging to their knowledge they are ever green,
whilst their rebel friends dance in shades of yellow and brown.

I see the cloud move past me.
As if they are in a rush to disuse a changeless blue sky into a
layering montage of white and greys.
What do those clouds seek?
Where do they so desperately want to reach?

Perhaps they follow the racing river,
towards a rushing sea to melt with a spreading ocean,
to go to...who knows where?

Is it for us to consider where?
Is this not the journey everything makes?

Is it not the truth that in each living,
breathing moment we are stepping into an abyss of unknowing,
Moving on a cycle of relentless change?

Is this not the ever changing energy of our breath?
None know if it shall be the first of more or the last.
To be is to change
And isn't change how we know we are life?

October 2014

Swallows

Sitting on the grass watching the Swallows dance in the long summer
light.

In the warm for this may.
As the clouds, due to injury seem to gather further away and the
space between them on the hill in the sky seems to clear.

As I sit and I watch a good friend.
Comes and draws near.

Sometime in 2021

<u>Wind</u>

The tree stands
Wind blows
Leaves move

October 2014

For Jayaraja

Stand! Victorious King!
Tell us we are free!

Are you not the man who sits with us in a room,
and asks for us to be silent;
So that we may discover that our voice can be the most valuable
weapon we posses?

Stand! Victorious King!
Teach us we are free!

Are you not the man who reads many books,
and learns all the questions;
So that you may have the knowledge to tell us that we already know
the answers we seek?

Stand! Victorious King!
Lead us to be free!

Are you not the man who walks in a crowd,
and loses his path;
So that we may see by following we only arrive at a destination we
ourselves do not need to go?

Stand! Victorious King!
Show us we are free!

Are you not the man who gave up on victory,
and the long valiant fight;
So that you could show us we are victorious too where there are no
losers on the quest with you to truth, knowledge and freedom?

Stand! Victorious King!
We are free!

October 2014

Stop!

Brothers and sisters I beg you to stop!
The wars and the hatred,
The judgement,
The lot!

Look deep in the mirror and what will you see?
Keep looking hard,
Your reflection
Is me!

October 2014

The Void & The Silence

The deafening silence of no people around.
The still of the floor,
No vibration from ground.
The still in the air,
When you're sitting alone.
The comfort of returning echo,
When everyone has gone.

The peace found in music,
When it's only you listening.
The comfort of warm light,
As evening candles are glistening.
The space of the void,
Where true meaning is found.
The beauty in silence,
With no pleasing around.

15.1.21

For Matthew

The man from my dreams,
Who's face I can't see,
Looks me deep in the eyes.

His eyes are like the reflection of sky
Over a deep dip in the ocean,
With twinkle stars at late twilight,
Where the sky lingers between blue and black.

His eyes meet mine and I melt.

The man from my dreams,
Who's lips I can't taste
Lingers at my mouth.

His taste is so sweet like granny's sweet home-baked cake,
Served with tea,
On your favourite plate with a spice and a heat
Like chilli dried in the midday sun.

His lips meet with mine and I quiver.

The man from my dreams,
Who's voice I can't hear
Whispers gently into my ear.

His voice is as comforting as an elder-down duvet,
On a snow day off,
when mum is there too and you sip a warm cup of cocoa
With Whipped cream on top.

His voice meets my ears and I burn.

The man from my dreams,
Who's scent I can't smell
Nuzzles in close to my nose.

His scent like droplets of morning dew in autumn,
Laying its claim over a warm golden landscape
With the last breath of flowers,
Drifting by in the breeze.

His scent meets my nose and I sigh.

The man from my dreams,
Who's body I can't feel,
Embraces my being with his.

His body is divine like a cluster of hills
With their strong solid peaks,
Followed by soft shallow valleys
And rocks that have settled in their perfect but random positions.

His body meets mine and I feel it.
I am awake.

October 2014

Marriage

To have and to hold
To own and to keep
To love and to cherish
To miss and to weep.
To want and to desire
To make and to perspire
To give and to honour
To worry and to sombre.

7.7.22

I think the world is like a big open book, we fill it with ourselves for others to look.

9.2.12

For The Loch

What is the Loch trying to tell me?

It ripples and plops as it rushes and meanders by.
It has no where to go.
So why does it move?

It listens to birdsong and waterfalls all day and night.

Raindrops tinkle and tickle at it's skin
As it shimmers and bounces in delight,
Softy being caressed,
Like a dance between the creator and the created.

Each tiny drop changes the vastness of the loch.

A mist hovers above,
Deciding whether to engulf the loch completely
As it softens at the edge of the shore.

There is a bright light spot coming from the depths of beneath.

How can this be?
Can the light really reach so far from beneath?
Or is it possible that the deep is so dark,
It had no choice but the reflect the light from the sky?

October 2014

Praying

My prayers have been answered
I see it each day.
It fills me with joy
I feel happy and gay.
Whatever I ask
I know God will answer.
With certainty I pray.
And will never falter.

2012

Cullen Skink

It was cold outside. Not an icy or frosty cold, more a heavy damp air several degrees below comfortable. The drizzle had soaked every part of me. My hair stuck to my head and water dripped down my face. I didn't care.

The walk had been exhilarating. As I stopped, I began to notice my hunger as a distant linger was caught in the air. An echo of other humans caught in the trees. The temptation of a hot cup of tea was too much to resist.

When I arrived at the cafe, presenting myself as a sodden pilgrim, the waitress looked at me with great concern. I ordered tea and Cullen Skink; Al fresco.

I sat, in the rain, at the side of the loch. Alone on the large deck, everyone else sat inside. Warm and comfortable. They chatted and laughed as they ate, the view passing them by.

I stared for a while as I watched and I wondered, Are they really looking? Do they see what they came to this cafe to see? Have they noticed the Loch floating by in all it's perfection? Have they noticed the mist in the hills? Do they see the ever changing colours of the trees as leaves dance with the wind?

Does it matter?

My attention drawn away to the warm steaming soup that arrived at my table and a different un-phased waitress who was concerned my bread would get damp. Not a concern as I ate it with delight admired by jealous gulls. My once warm tea cooling in the sticky, damp air.

No one asked me why I sat alone and ate outside in the rain. Some people did watch me, I felt their eyes. Some even laughed, I felt their smiles.

I was at peace, just sitting there, listening, to the Loch. Hearing the stories it had to tell me. I was eaves dropping on a conversation between water, wind and rain, a communication between land, trees and birds. There was so much to hear out there, in the quiet.

The Loch had so much to say. All it's knowing, sharing with me so generously.

As I sat there quiet enough to hear it. I became part of the sound. The endless din of mindless chatter from inside couldn't penetrate the triple glazed windows.

Bliss.

October 2014

For Matthew Part 2

The emptiness.
A fog slowly engulfing the view
Creeping around
Little by little
Thickening, Swelling
Expanding, Growing.
The emptiness.
Making everything seem unclear
It blurs and bends
Reality by feelings
Morphing, Moulding
Blocking, Exaggerating,
The emptiness.
Such vivid brutal pain
Stabs and burns
Repairing by breaking
Poking, Prodding
Piercing, Tearing
The emptiness,
After you.

June 16th 2015
(Matthew's Birthday)

-It is better to have loved and lost, than to have never loved at all.
Apparently.

Is the chapter over?
The song has been sung,
the melody had barely begun being written.
Sometimes a jingle can convey a more clearer message.

<u>For The Tree</u>

Thoughts of the world
Sat by a tree,
Revealing my dreams
It gets to know me.

Keeping my secrets,
Telling no lies,
The tree is beside me,
It won't leave my side.

October 2014

Wonder in the Woods

When other people walk in the woods,
I wonder what they see.
Do they see personality and a future friend
Or do they just see a tree?

Do they see drama, sins and greek tragedies
or epic sagas, comedy and magical fantasies?
Do they notice the stories, cheap lusts and warm friendly embraces
Or do they notice expressions in contortions and small, hidden faces?

Do they hear symphonies, a chorus and beautiful singing choirs?
Do they listen to crunching, rustling and the cracking of fires?
Can they hear conversations, catchups and friendly chatter
Or do they repulse at sounds of gossip, squabbling and annoying,
bitter chatter?

I wonder if others feel the same as I am.
When I am in the woods I feel equal.
As strong as I can.

Do others feels strong when they walk in the woods
Or do they feel intimidated, frightened nervous and shook?
Do they see horrors, get chills and sense sorrows?
Can they see war zones, pains and unresolved traumas?

Do others see cycles of death and rebirth?
Do they consider the impact each creature has on the earth?
Do other people find deep grateful solace and
do they also love to walk alone in the forrest?

I wonder what people see in the trees?
I wonder if they see the same wonders as me?

17.4.2020

Mental health issues come from two disconnections;
Disconnection from nature,
Disconnection from the moment.

14.10.18

A Covid Christmas

Empty buses driving by,
Big full moon beaming in the sky.
Twinkle lights in the distance, glisten.
Standing alone in silence just listening.
What a year it has been,
The one with the virus.
Where we all got locked up with no one beside us.

In a world where love,
Has become about protecting a stranger,
Spending Christmas alone,
And New Year out of danger.

30.12.20

Me As You

Why do I have to be like someone else?
When actually, I really like being like myself.
I may not be perfect,
I am very much flawed,
Does that mean I deserve to be ignored?

Why do I have to live as you say?
When I enjoy doing things my particular way.
It may bot be the best,
I might even be wrong,
Does that really mean I should silence my song?

Why do I have to walk the same path?
When honestly, I prefer to make my own track.
It may not be easy,
It might even cause me pain,
Does that mean I should bloc all the wisdom I'd gain?

Why do I have to pretend to be the same?
When pretending is exhausting again and again.
I may not be normal,
I am very much odd,
Does that really make me a weird and worthless sod?

17.3.21

Mainstreamers – A Musing

It crossed my mind, for the first time today, there are people who think governance is a good idea.
This is keeps them safe and they trust it.

It must be a pleasant space to be in, regardless of it's truth.

To trust government seems impossible for me. Maybe it comes down to parenting, schooling and our relationship with authority.

It must be nice to have that. I have never trusted mine or it in my life so it is hard for me to imagine an honest, trustworthy authority.

It must be nice to have the weight of taking care of yourself released. The have lesser of an enemy. To feel safe. Right or not, true or not, ignorance and faith are bliss.

There are people the system works for. People who fit and don't have to compromise. For some the system makes sense and is to be protected. Some people have never had reason to question its validity, never suffered at the hands of it.

The mainstreamers.

16.4.20

Free To Be Me

I live as myself,
The only way that I know.
It makes me feel happy,
It helps me to grow.
I do not need your guidance,
I don't want advice.
I just want consideration,
My way could be alright.
Human amongst humans,
I want freedom to exist.
If I wasn't a part of life,
My part would be missed.
I know I am important,
Nature brought me here.
My existence, my way,
My version of life, I hold dear.

17.3.21

Life...Living

Each moment in the day,
Breathing,
Heart beating,
Time passes.

Walking in nature,
Being,
Stepping,
Watching grasses.

17.3.21

This Woman

Who am I
This Woman
Who lies in my bed?

How am I
This Woman
Who lives in my head?

For am I
This Woman
Who bleeds and is red?

But am I
This Woman
Who lives and is dead?

7.7.22

TheBreath of Courage

The warning in my heart,
Making me wrong.
The lump in my throat,
Silences my song.
The fear in my feet,
Quiets my voice.
The judgement behind my eyes,
Removing my choice.
The breath from the air,
Courage to feel.

17.3.21

Longing For Love

Sitting down here,
Resting in my chair,
Not feeling alone,
But wishing you were there.

Someone who cares,
To listen to my day,
Not to judge me,
But hearing the words I say.

Wanting a connection,
Content here alone,
No rush on things,
But I'm missing that you're gone.

Feeling the space,
Empty by my side,
Not to fill it mindlessly,
But longing for words to collide.

14.3.21

<u>I Am</u>

I know who I am,
I know what i've done,
I know where I'm headed,
I know where I've gone.
I know where I've been,
I know what I've seen,
I know who I am,
I know I am me.

18.4.20

Life

Consciousness,
Awareness,
Discernment,
The destiny is death.
Love is the journey.

18.4.20

Dreamers Vision

As the light shine falls away,
Dreamers vision a brand new day.
Lovers magic through the night,
Haters havoc pain and fight.

What becomes of those that breathe,
The ones who hurt from sweet relief.
Us who make the world are one,
We together, fuller, strong.

Maybe dreams are just a wish,
A place to imagine, float and drift.
Or what is dreams are paths to take,
What if goals are ours to make.

Now is the time for all that we have,
Making future, creating plans.
Living life of blind and death,
Heart eyes open, they see the rest.

Feel your heart, beyond what's there.
Day to day living a blinding stare.
Love is just a thought away,
Dream to live it, a brighter day.

It seems obvious to me that crop circles are created by Gaia, not aliens.

15.5.20

<u>Grief</u>

Grief unspoken
Tears not a waterfall
Guilt in heart

October 2014

Death – A Musing

I think we are urgently attracted to death.
We love the smell of decomposition.
We are drawn to it.
We are drawn to death, always.
It allures us.

It in it's infinite appealing.
We resist it because we want it so badly.
So we learn to fear it.
The battle between pain and the chaos of existence.
Versus the nothingness of non-existence.
It is our dance.

Our repulsion to death has caused us to seek many ways to avoid it's
allure.
Ultimately though, we are always trying to find out way back to
nothingness.
The stillness of calm.
It is the effort we must put in order to exist that pains us.
Death is the welcoming letting go of all that effort.

15.5.20

The Girl

The girl who was never written,
Became the woman who's story was told.
Who feared her world would be known,
That lived a life that was bold.

This creature who was never sure,
A wonder who always dared to know.
From a place nobody considered,
A complex and fair way to grow old.

7.7.22

Mastering self is power.
Mastering others is stress!

5.4.21

Life Through A Lens

I felt so little in my life that I had to devote my time to capturing what I perceived as beauty. To try and invoke some sort of feeling, because I didn't believe it was there. I wanted to capture it, hold on to it because I didn't believe it was meant for me or that it could be mine.

Now I have feeling in my life I spend less time trying to capture it. I understand that what I perceive through a lens will never come close to the experience of living it.

4.9.19

Sometimes...

Sometimes I'm fat,
Sometimes I'm thin,
I want someone to love me,
The person within.

Sometimes I'm happy,
Sometimes I'm sad,
I want someone to love me,
Through good and bad.

Sometimes I'm crazy,
Sometimes I'm sane,
I want someone to love me,
Help relieve my pain.

Sometimes I laugh,
Sometimes I cry,
I want someone to love me,
Who loves to know why.

Sometimes I'm lazy,
Sometimes I'm fast,
I want someone to love me,
Who sees beyond my past.

Sometimes I'm caring,
Sometimes I'm mean,
I want someone to love me,
Who is on my team.

Sometimes life is serious,
Sometimes it's a game,
I'll find someone who loves me,
And I'll love them the same.

Sometime in 2014 (likely)

I've Found Love

The love I have found
can never be taken,
The love I have found
Can not be mistaken.
The love I have found
Can do me no wrong,
The love I have found
Will never be gone.

The love I have found
Will always be mine,
The love I have found
Will make sure i'm fine.
The love I have found
Does not have a limit,
The love I have found
Brings joy in a minute.

The love I have found
Is as golden as silence,
The love I have found
Gives me good guidance.
The love I have found
Brings peace to my heart,
The love I have found
Will never depart.

The love I have found
Will stay with me forever,
The love I have found
Will not give up, ever.

The love I have found
Comes directly from God,
The love I have found
Makes my loveless life odd.

9.2.12

Thoughts

I think about life
All the moments I've had
The struggles and strains
The good and the bad.

I think about love a
All the people I meet
The energy it took
To get back on my feet.

I think about honour
And all that it means
To work all together
Alone or in teams

I think of my family
Acquaintance and friends
All I must do
To try make a mends.

I think of the joy
This journey could bring
I know that my truth
Must come from within.

2012

The Chrysalis

The chrysalis
Is warm
and safe
and dark.
Where I lose myself
and fall apart.
To become a
Version I was
Meant to be.
Known by God
But not
to me.

7.7.22

Candle Light

Here I write in candle light
By the hand of God
In the dark of night.
Stars appear above my head,
Stay, watching as I pray.

My heart is filled with warmth and love
As I write messages from above.
For this gift I am truly grateful,
As I sit writing
By candle light at my table.

The thoughts and ideas come through my head
Full of hope and joy
For me to spread.

The word of love bringing peace to mankind
The gospel of God
For them to find.
Their meaning of life
To save their soul.

God I am promised has only one goal
To help each and other
And be a good friend.
Live in life and truth
Be love until the end.

2.3.12

I Am A Woman

I am a woman
I have a womb
I make dreams come true
When I talk to the moon.

I am a woman
I have subtle breast
I make insatiable magic
That won't let me rest.

I am a woman
I have unique power
I make miracles happen
When I unfold like a flower.

I am a woman
I have an obvious weakness
I make men afraid
They they attack my meekness.

28.10.21

Rage and Burn

The rage I feel at what they did and has been done.
The anger burns me deeply,
Intense like the sun.
Anything I say or do, how I respond or feel.
Always questioned by others; Is this real?

Who decided is I am right or wrong?
Certainly not a stranger
Who is there, then gone.
Why is my view never accepted?
Always assumed that it's wrong; I'm less than.

I make no mistake in expressing what I see.
It makes no difference
What you think of me.
But defending abuse and the harm that is causes.
Denying the effects of rape; Harms our daughters.

I don't blame you for denying or fearing the burn.
But it's not me who needs changed,
Only them.
The ones who dismiss the effect they have on others.
The ones who stay quiet; Defending their brothers.

I'll never sit down and accept it's okay.
I'm not stupid enough
To think it will just go away.
I won't silence myself or numb my reaction.
I am here to burn it up; Cause decisive action.

16.1.22

Finding Truth

Sometimes you need to leave everything you know to truly find yourself. As you exist outside of all you have experienced before, you become who you truly are.

When they ides of humanity becomes secondary to the pure soul that seeks to understand and experience. And then you return to all you once knew. You realise you were only what you had been taught to become.

You never really existed outside of perceptions of others ideas of you. You never knew who you were. No one really knowing who you are. Aside from the ground that felt your changing weight and the air that recycled each rejected breath of your slumber.

7.7.22

The Man

The man who I still do not know
Who compels my waking dreams
He command my life of desire
As the master of all it can be.

A promise of tone and form precise
The idea that won't go away
To me, I am under his power forever
To him I am a breeze he feels but can't see.

7.7.22

Unfair Games

Unfair games we play
With unwritten rules
In codes that are unclear
And commands that ring untrue.

Words that can move in the spell of it,
Lives that are crushed in the wake.
When no one dare speak of the truth of it
And mistakes can never be made.

7.7.22

Fear

Feeling afraid
Do not know why
Looking, seeing, knowing.

October 2014

Joyless or Alive

Joyless or alive
What will it be
Live a performance
For everyone to see
Be as expected
No fault is allowed
Fun is a luxury
If it pleases the crowd
Live life as desired
Not as it rings true
Be here to please others
Forget about you.

7.7.22

Life As Art

My life is an artwork
Who would deny it
Those who reject art
Have never really tried it.

To live as a masterpiece
And forge a tapestry
To become an unfolding
Of whatever we were meant to be.

Living as a wonder
Who proves it is not.
Those who don't hear music
Or dance when it is hot.

While real living is for
The bold and the brave
The art is in the expression
And a willingness to play.

Life is a sculpture
That is built and decays
Who's wonder is witnessed
Through the passage of days.

No one can decide
If their beauty is seen
For the artist and artwork
Are collaborative team.

The living only produces
A story to tell
But the author can not demand
That the reader do it well.

The trust and the faith
In the beauty that unfolds
Fear the risk of a story
To the great never told.

As the artist, the artwork
The muse and the canvas
In the light that runs through us
Around and surrounds us.

For life is for living
And art is the experience
The mastering of living it
And wandering where life leads us.

7.7.22

Photography Musing

I was a photographer because I wanted to capture the beauty I saw in the world and share it with others. I stopped because people couldn't see what I saw and sometimes saw ugliness instead.

Now, I realise that those that seek beauty in the world seek it and find it regardless of me trying to show it. Those that don't won't, no matter what I showed them.

Date Unknown

Poetry In Motion

Poems that stream
From no particular source.
Words that just flow
Without judgement or remorse.
No form or pretence
Or anything they are not.
Just words on a page
Where they mean a lot.

7.7.22

Allowing

Letting go
Letting know
Letting flow

October 2014

Heart Stone

This rock that I love
That was given a gift
Broke a piece of my heart
When it went adrift.

My heart stone I loved
A Treasure so dear
I miss surely knowing
It is no longer near.

7.7.22

Angels

The angels that watch over my bed at night,
Come in peace and love
And warm white light.

They bring me strength to work through my day,
Helping and guiding
And guarding my way.

The angels of love help me deal with my pain,
Bringing comfort and joy
And I don't feel the same.

They bring me hope and i'll trust them forever,
It stays with me always
And each and any endeavour.

2012

Growing Pains

It's mistakes that we learn from
As painful as it is.
No way to bypass
The reality of this.

We try and we dodge
In any way to avoid.
But it is the growth that's required.
To fill the deep void.

It hurts when it happens
And we fear it unfold
But whats worse than sad endings
Is a story never told.

7.7.22

Sleep Time

I'd like to sleep,
But my mind think it's funny.
To make up these poems
Imagining it'll make money.
When more likely what will happen,
Is no one will bother reading,
An all I have done is wasted
Good sleep I was needing.

7.7.22

<u>Suicide</u>

The hardest thing about surviving suicide, is knowing it doesn't offer a way out.

7.7.22

The Cocoon

In the darkness lies our power,
Of true transformation.
As we give up all we were,
And we are tortured by waiting.

The deepest change takes time,
A limited commodity for a human.
But if you're not transforming,
What are you doing?

In the shadows you'll find,
The key to that change.
In the mess that will follow,
And the process of feeling deranged.

We must lose our minds,
Our hearts and ourselves.
To truly know it's value
When we create it again.

You can not change,
With the light of the seen.
There is no point in cleansing,
What is already clean.

Our challenge for change,
Is to be true to all life.
To know that nothing grows,
Without struggle or strife.

Transformation is easy,
If you willingly take on the challenge.
It's what we are designed for,
Something all humans can manage.

7.7.22

Epilogue

This book ends with an intention that you gained something from reading it.

My writing, my expression now part of my survival I likely would not be alive without as I learn to release the energy that moves through me, constantly.

Thank you for reading and witnessing this energy expressed through these words.

Blessings to you and yours!

I would like to end with a passage of expression that I intend to be part of another book...

This is my introduction of Phoenix Earth.

Phoenix Earth

As I experience the sorrow and heart felt despair. Reading stories of fleeing refugees and their gratitude of those that survived, I could not help but realise; Not a single person on this planet today can claim to be neither the persecuted nor the persecutor.

We all have a part and connection to the horror of our one human race. Genocide, war, ethnic cleansing, subscription.

We have all suffered.

We can choose to end this suffering with the acknowledgement non of us are free from this past.

We are one.

In the westernised society I live in, today it is fair to note man changes have taken place to the traditional introduction of the patriarchy. We are currently not governed by a patriarchal system. However, the control of patriarchy is ever evident in our systems and belief, pushed by old ways.

The generations of youth are abolishing these notions, slowly. And through time the age of tradition fights against it with the strong hold of reason and logic. It is a battle to find the balance and tolerance that will be the Phoenix Earth.

It is not about overthrowing a system that is done. It is about overthrowing the mind restrictions the system had fed into us that are the underlying the core values of our society.

It is calling out how many ways the feminine and masculine is over-exerted and demonised so that we may not find the beauty in all of it through the denial of any of it.

Science has caused many of the problems our planet currently faces. Science will not give us the answers we seek to save ourselves.
Only nature can.

By handing back control to nature can the Earth be free to repair our damage. No matter how hard we try to fix as humans we can only ever interfere. Our arrogance is now so outstanding it seems we need a miracle to allow us to survive.

I recall hearing the sound of the last ever call of a male bird (who's species name alludes my memory) seeking his mate. A species driven to extinction as the BBC intervened and recorded his call that would never ear a response.
A being seeking love and finding nothing. He would have died alone, never understanding his mate would never come no matter how hard he tried or how beautiful his call. He would never understand that his death and the death of every single one of his kin was caused by our science.
Or perhaps, he did understand and chose to call regardless. A call that would likely never be heard by the ignorance and greed of humans who must expand. Humans who always need more. Who must control, dominate, who must interfere.

I openly wept.

I wept for us. I wept for his loss. I wept for the grief he will never feel. I wept for the sadness and plight we have brought to the other beings of the earth. I wept to release my karma in my part of it all.

I felt their pain, to release it and ours forever by speaking the despair and allowing the recovery.

I wept for my guilt.

Science and the pursuit of proof is the ultimate form of human arrogance. Big business and it's need for accumulation is the ultimate form of human greed.

Before science decided it could figure out all the answers we never dared to assume we could understand everything.
Children playing God. It is not for us to judge and control life, yet now we have billions of little gods wreaking havoc upon our Earth.

The theoretical discovery of dark matter bridging us full circle to the understanding that we already once had... That there is an energy that can not be defined that binds us all to one another.

An energy that can not be quantified nor explained. An energy that must exist to make sense of creation. An energy that can not be measured but keeps us all in bind.

This energy has many names.

I call it God.

If God will mould us to the destiny of creation, why must we play a part? As we are in the play of it all, observed, the observer, the witness and the fool. We are heading to where wherever we will go for creation to develop itself as we become part of our own destruction.

About The Author

Terri Lee-Shield is a designer, artist, activist and author from County Durham in the North East UK. Born in 1983 she has always been creative working and studying in the creative industry since leaving school in 1999.

A survivor of abuse, rape and a serious of unfortunate experiences she uses her unique insight and way of seeing the wold to create life affirming systems.

With a strong intuition and a deep connection to spirit and the natural world she expresses her creativity and artistry through several forms of media.

A word from the author...

"I am a conscious creator and I express my ideas, designs and understanding of nature and our natural systems through different forms of expression.

Following an organic exploration I have uncovered natural, holistic solutions to many of our man made problems.

My books express these discoveries and present the understandings I have gained in different forms of media. From self help to mutual support and relationships to exploring the patterns and energetic dynamics of humanity through story form.

I have a particular interest in trauma, evolution and our human nature as spiritual beings connected through physicality and the reproductive nature of life.

My goal is to express ways of healing and creating more effective, holistic, life-affirming systems that benefit individuals, humanity and our relationship with nature."

Find out more about Terri at:

www.snowdropssunsets.co.uk

Printed in Great Britain
by Amazon

83278549R00058